the tao of numbers

the tao of numbers

poems by

Erik Richardson

Cover photo by Juan Salamanca
Cover image by Zen GrayWhite

ISBN: 978-1-63980-314-9

Kelsay Books
502 South 1040 East, A-119
American Fork, Utah 84003
Kelsaybooks.com

For Emery, Sean, Madisen, Brady, and so many other wondrous students over the years who taught me what counts.

Acknowledgments

Chapters 6, 7, and 8 first appeared in *Stoneboat Literary Journal,* issue 6-2, 2016

Chapter 2 first appeared in *Blue Heron Review,* issue 13, 2021

Contents

For chapter x, page number is:
$$f(x) = x + 10$$

1

the set that can be counted is not the undivided set.
named only by negation.
the beginning of number is the undivided
since no subset has been carved out.
zero is the set of all things
the flowing river
the unsliced bread
the world to a newborn child.

2

people think that by finding one group countable
other groups are greater than or less than.
they name this long and that short.
this child ahead and that behind.
the even better than the odd.
let the sage erase boundaries and limits
seeing each student as not yet
instead of only
open instead of closed.
let her show the student she always counts
and she will keep on counting.

3

exalt not the ending number
but the difference from beginning to end
naming the high score as beautiful
labels a low score as ugly.
if we count from 50 to 75 think of the adventure
the landscape of numbers we have crossed
but if 89 walks next door to 90,
he is hailed as a hero.
where is the journey? the tension?
what graceful curve has the arc of his character scribed?

4

numbers cannot stand apart
they lose their meaning without context
95. what does that mean?
yields nothing.
holds nothing.
what does it reflect of the universe?
so many sets it could belong to
numbers whose digits sum to 14
multiples of 5
products of two primes
a single snowflake is not a day off school.

5

the spirit of counting moves through the undivided set.
having no particular end goal
it is infinite.
by not clinging to each number
polishing it and putting it on a plaque on the wall
or branding it on the forehead of a student
she remains a part of the group
the numbers she reached before do not define her
any more than 71 defines 101.
her counting is timeless and what came before is swallowed
with her tongue always reaching for the whispered sound
of the next number in her journey.

6

counting is like water
flowing over and under all things
numbers ripple and jump downstream
taking us through canyons and prairies
the white foam fractions splashing over
the edge of our canoe
they trickle like rain down through soil
and up to leaftips
they drift down like fractal snowflakes
sprinkling students making them laugh.
the sage leaves space for splashing
for building lopsided snowmen
for snow angels.

7

each child can only swim so fast
through the river of numbers.
the sage allows for that
if she pulls them too hard
she will be exhausted
they will be exhausted
let them float on their backs
spitting little fountains of numbers
or blow underwater rings
like porpoises
let them drift at night
counting stars overhead.

8

in learning to carve out subsets
and count their members
can you remember they are written in water
not stone?
can you breathe and let them disappear
back into the undivided set?
in numbering the notes in a birdsong
on a summer evening
can you let go of wishing it were a different bird,
a different song?

9

a class is made one by the idea
they are joined around the undiscovered
helping each other like reals
gradually carving out subsets as they travel
toward the undivided future
counting on each other
to be open to new questions
never thinking themselves finished
never thinking the others finished
like infinite sets.

10

if she thinks of her number as part of a larger stream
she will be able to laugh
when she goes through the rapids.

11

imagined but unable to be counted
that is the infinite set
with zero things carved out
but containing all things
that is the undivided
you cannot cling to one part of this river
to hold it still.
or lift out one handful of water
and say it is better than the rest.

12

if the sage can let go of thinking
one number is better than another
she can be impartial like the rain.
if she can be impartial like the rain
she can nourish all the wildflowers
if she can nourish all the wildflowers
they will see that they cannot define themselves
as real, but instead cling to the *i*,
the quantum of imagination
that makes them all complex.

13

when the students lose their curiosity
arise rules and deadlines
when rules and deadlines arise
there come conformity and consequence
the sage will offer those two tyrants
a snowball straight to the chest
and the students will remember how to laugh.

14

let go of thinking high numbers are better than low numbers.
drop the labels "fast" or "slow" in the river
and as they sink your students will float.

15

if you only ever celebrate goals
you disparage the process:
destinations, the journey,
rest stops, the struggle
with all its points of inflection
yourself, others,
you erase away too much—
all the area under the curve.

16

the sage who truly understands
is content to leave some things uncounted
undivided
some assignments ungraded
the source is both zero and infinite
remember the handful of river.

17

the undivided set is hard to define
yet in it are all possible subsets
even the subset of all sets
that do not contain themselves.
though it cannot be counted,
it is the source of all counting.
just so, the student can never be
measured completely
each a diagonal proof.

18

numbers cannot be divided.
we forget this all too often.
groups of things in the world can be carved out
and they can be carved again into smaller groups
where the things are still there.
but as soon as you divide 9, it is
as gone as the morning dew by noon.
the curve will always elude the grasp
of infinite rectangles with their sharp little elbows
and ankles.

19

a student cannot be divided.
as soon as he is carved out from the group,
he has shrunk to be something less than he was.
and each part we measure,
each set of skills we carve out from the rest
is, like a fractal, also smaller than it was before
and also immeasurable.
it is like trying to measure a coastline
or the magnified edge of a snowflake.
we can never hold imagination still
so we can never quite capture the whole
in a two-dimensional world.

20

the sage revels in the coincidence
of coffee cups and donuts
sometimes she makes snow angels
but does not give reasons
the sage does not argue one snow angel
is better than another
or this number is better than that one.

21

the student who is as equally amazed
by small numbers as by large
has grasped the truth
like one who values the beginning of the river
as much as the middle
if she can appreciate the undivided zero
as the source of wonder
then she has grasped infinity.

22

the student who is aware
of competitive comparison and conflict
but chooses curiosity instead
approaches the undivided
the student who resists carving herself out
remains larger.

23

the sage does not count for glory
she does not count for show
or self
or money.
she counts because it is wondrous in itself
she does not teach others to count for glory
or show
or self
or money.

24

the undivided set is infinite
you can carve it into pieces, but they flow on
gone in a gurgle of the flowing stream.
leaving you with empty placeholders.

25

once we carve each student out from the group
and label one better or faster
they shrink to become as separate rivers
and no longer see they are flowing to the same sea.

26

pure counting exploring the undivided set
it cannot be named by any subset
it is without limits like a child's mind
exploring the numbered axes in all directions
with crayons too fat and happy to ever draw lines
between big and small.

27

in the creative mind
there is no curve that traces the border
between real and imaginary
let us subtract one, let that mean the carved out, the separate
what is a square root of that?
what must be multiplied against itself
to be reabsorbed into zero—the set of all things?
perhaps separateness.
we must create a fusion
the illusion that self is separate from the whole
and must be crashed at accelerated particle speeds
into the illusion that illusions-are-separate-from-reality.

28

this is not the end
for these children
as raindrops
and sky-diving snowflakes
breathe out a trail of numbers
falling back into the whole
the undivided
and when the sage has taught them
to un-count, un-carve,
they play like porpoises blowing bubble rings,
flap snow angels into existence.
this is also not the beginning.

About the Author

Erik Richardson is a former math teacher who now works as a freelance journalist and political consultant living in Mexico, Missouri. He and his wife also run a small company developing e-learning and engaged storytelling tools for businesses around the country. His poetry has appeared in a variety of journals and anthologies over the years, with his first published collection, *a berserker stuck in traffic,* published in 2014, and his second chapbook, *song of ourself,* in 2017.

www.ingramcontent.com/pod-product-compliance
Lightning Source LLC
Chambersburg PA
CBHW030815090426
42737CB00010B/1290